Dr. Fry's

Instant Words Bingo

A Game for Learning Instant Words

by Edward Fry, Ph.D.

Teacher Created Materials, Inc.
6421 Industry Way
Westminster, CA 92683
www.teachercreated.com

ISBN-0-7439-3523-3

©2003 by Teacher Created Materials, Inc.
Made in U.S.A.

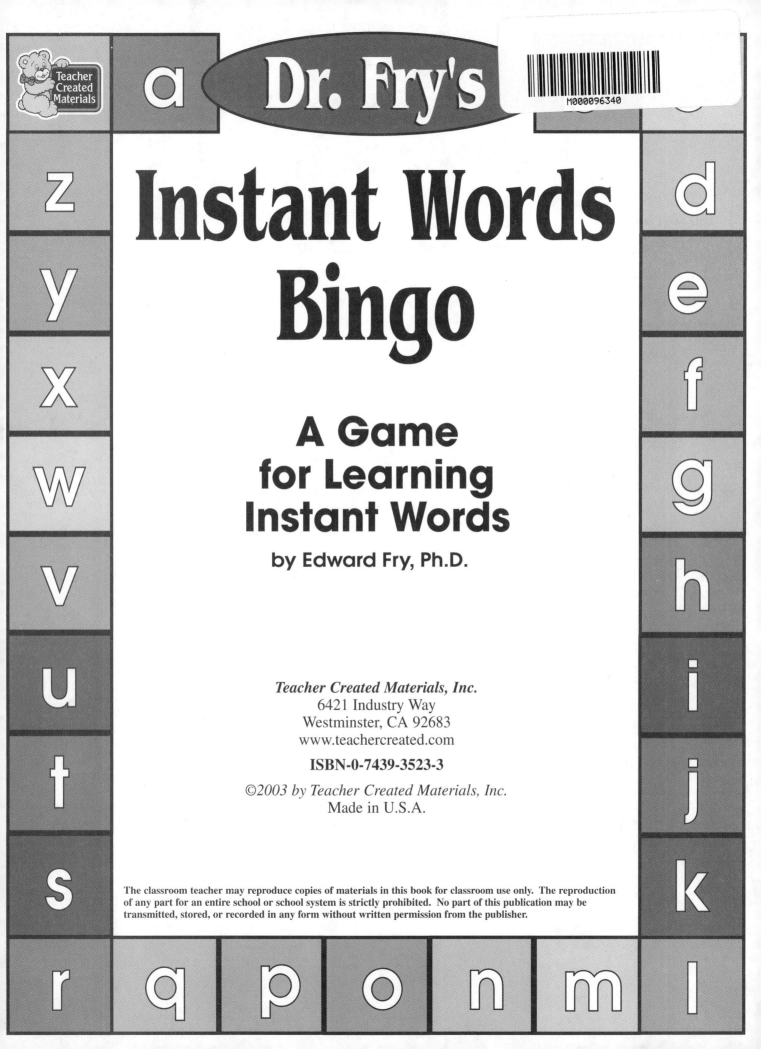

Table of Contents

Introduction

Instant Words Bingo Cards

This book contains 100 Bingo cards accompanied with directions and teaching instructions. These cards teach the first 100 Instant Words, which are the most commonly-used words in reading and writing. They account for 50% of all the words in an average book. Because they are repeated so often, students need to recognize them "instantly." This game will help teach these high-frequency words, which are important to reading fluency. In fact, it is impossible to read a page of any text without knowing at least some (certainly the first 25) of the Instant Words.

The cards in this book can be duplicated for one class. You will need a different card for each student. There are four sets of cards in this book, so there are four different Bingo games. Note that the teacher should use only one set of Bingo cards at a time. There are 25 different cards for each set, allowing the game to be played by up to 25 students. The Directions section is repeated at the beginning of each set of 25 Bingo cards. The four sets teach the first 100 Instant Words as noted below.

Set A—25 different cards for Instant Words 1–25   Set C—25 different cards for Instant Words 51–75
Set B—25 different cards for Instant Words 26–50   Set D—25 different cards for Instant Words 76–100

Round 1: Regular Bingo

This instructional game works like a regular Bingo game.

1. The teacher calls out a word.
2. The student uses a pencil to cross through the word (square) on his or her individual Bingo card.
3. The first student to get five words in a row wins.

Round 2: Diagnostic Bingo

After the first round is finished, the second round is to be played.

1. Tell the students this is a game to be played on their own—no helping each other.
2. The teacher keeps calling words until nearly all the squares are marked off.
3. The teacher omits two words (squares).
4. The teacher now looks over the students' Bingo cards and checks to see if only those two words are unmarked.
5. If so, all those students win round two.

Individual Records and Teaching Needs

The teacher now has a written record of which words the student can correctly read. The blank squares show which words the student needs to learn (not counting the two words the teacher intentionally omitted). This is not a totally accurate test of word recognition, but it does give a good indication of what words each student needs to learn.

The Bingo cards can now be used as individualized study sheets since they show which words (the unmarked squares) the student needs to learn. The marked sheets can also be taken home to show parents or guardians evidence of learning and which words need to be practiced.

(*Note:* The Instant Words, while very important, are far from a complete reading program. The words and this Bingo game should be taught in conjunction with a balanced reading program which includes plenty of reading practice in books, many writing opportunities, listening, phonics, fluency, and all of the other reading skills.)

Introduction (cont.)

Ideas for Teaching the Instant Words

A study in a K–2 school, in an area that had a majority of Spanish-surnamed students, used a balanced reading program. They included in their program an emphasis on learning the Instant Words through flashcards, games, reading, and writing lessons. The school had a reward system in which they gave a certificate for students who could read a basic number of Instant Words and a T-shirt for students who could read a significant number of Instant Words. The following are the achievement levels by grade and the percentage of students who reached those levels by the end of the grade:

Kindergarten

Certificate Level	50 words	45% of students
T-shirt Level	100 words	20% of students

Grade 1

Certificate Level	150 words	76% of students
T-shirt Level	200 words	36% of students

Grade 2

Certificate Level	300 words	77% of students
T-shirt Level	400 words	64% of students

Additional Resources for Teaching the Instant Words

The Instant Words and other helpful information are also available in the following Dr. Fry products, published by Teacher Created Materials.

- TCM 2757—*1000 Instant Words*
  The basic word list is in large type and includes teaching suggestions and 100 picture nouns.

- TCM 2760—*How to Teach Reading*
  This is a basic instruction manual for teachers, parents, and aides that integrates methods for teaching the Instant Words with phonics, comprehension, and writing.

- TCM 2661 and TCM 2662—*Instant Words Flashcards*
  These sturdy flash cards are suitable for group or individual instruction, games, and pocket charts. (Set A has 50 Instant Words, and Set B has 50 more Instant Words.)

- TCM 3503—*Instant Word Practice Book*
  This book is full of Instant Word reproducible work sheets, word search games, and other activities. Twenty units teaches the 200 Instant Words.

- TCM 2750—*Spelling Book: Words Most Needed Plus Phonics*
  This is a complete spelling curriculum for grades 1–6 in 195 weekly lessons that teaches the spelling of 3000 Instant Words plus phonic skills and word study for classrooms and remedial or tutoring instruction.

- TCM 2758—*Word Book for Beginning Writers*
  This is a student reference book to be used like a dictionary for quickly looking up the spelling of the 1000 Instant Words with ample room for the student to add personal words.

Set A: Instant Words 1–25

the ✓	in ✓	he	as	at ✓
of	is ✓	was	with	be
and ✓	you	for	his	this ✓
a ✓	that	on	they	have
to	it	are	I ✓	from

Directions

1. Duplicate one Bingo card for each student. Each student needs a different Bingo card, but all Bingo cards must be from the same set.

2. Call out the words in the word list above in any order—first to last, then at another time last to first, etc.

3. As you call each word, use it in a sentence or phrase, then repeat the word.

4. Ask the students to mark an **X** on top of each word that is called.

5. Allow sufficient time for the students to search for the word on their Bingo cards before saying the next word.

6. Remember to omit two words if you are using the game for diagnosis. (See Round 2: Diagnostic Bingo on page 3.) As the students learn the words, the rate of calling out the words can be increased.

When you are teaching beginning readers, you can write the word on the board or hold up a flash card containing the word so the students can make a visual match. The same Instant Words are available on flash cards from Teacher Created Materials or at educational school supply stores, or you can make your own flash cards. After students become more familiar with the Instant Words, you can just call out the words (without writing on the board or using flash cards).

Do not proceed to the next set until most of the students have learned the majority of the words. Generally speaking, Set C and Set D are too advanced for kindergarten. However, all sets are suitable for first grade, second grade, and remedial or ELL students.

Save the student cards for individualized instruction, a record of progress, and take-home evidence of learning.

the	of	and	a	to
in	is	you	that	it
he	was	for	on	are
as	with	his	they	I
at	be	this	have	from

from	the	of	and	a
to	in	is	you	that
it	he	was	for	on
are	as	with	his	they
I	at	be	this	have

at	as	he	in	the
be	with	was	is	of
this	his	for	you	and
have	they	on	that	a
are	it	I	from	to

Dr. Fry's Instant Words Bingo

Card A-4

SET **A**

Instant Words 1–25

this	his	for	you	and
a	that	on	they	have
of	is	was	with	be
the	in	he	as	at
it	are	to	I	from

they	on	that	a	of
is	be	with	was	have
and	you	for	this	his
to	I	from	it	are
he	as	at	in	the

with	from	I	they	his
this	at	be	as	are
for	on	was	he	it
you	that	is	in	to
and	have	the	of	a

that	he	it	was	on
for	as	are	with	his
I	they	be	at	have
this	from	you	the	of
to	and	a	is	in

in	at	be	as	that
for	I	this	to	and
from	they	he	a	you
are	it	is	the	with
was	of	have	his	on

of	is	a	and	from
on	you	the	as	be
his	they	I	are	it
to	with	this	that	at
have	for	was	in	he

and	a	that	on	they
have	this	be	at	as
he	in	with	you	for
are	I	of	to	was
it	is	from	the	his

I	are	it	be	as
the	you	on	from	and
a	is	of	at	that
this	with	to	have	for
was	in	he	they	his

Dr. Fry's Instant Words Bingo

Card A-12

Instant Words 1–25

his	on	to	have	of
for	with	they	you	is
a	the	was	this	I
and	as	are	in	that
from	be	it	he	at

as	I	they	his	with
this	be	at	from	have
it	that	you	is	in
are	on	for	was	he
to	a	and	of	the

Dr. Fry's Instant Words Bingo

Card A-14

SET **A**

Instant Words 1–25

and	you	for	his	this
have	they	on	that	a
from	I	are	it	to
at	as	in	he	the
with	be	was	of	is

© Teacher Created Materials, Inc   #3523 Instant Words Bingo

Dr. Fry's Instant Words Bingo

is	he	they	are	and
you	on	it	the	to
that	for	his	a	this
have	in	from	I	was
be	as	with	at	of

be	from	have	this	at
to	I	are	it	they
on	that	a	his	as
you	and	for	of	is
was	with	the	in	he

it	are	the	in	at
as	he	to	a	from
his	for	this	you	and
be	is	with	have	was
I	of	that	on	they

was	is	with	of	be
his	for	this	you	and
on	they	have	that	to
a	are	it	from	I
he	as	in	at	the

for	his	this	you	and
a	that	on	they	have
at	as	he	in	the
of	is	be	with	was
are	I	to	from	it

on	they	is	and	to
he	as	at	in	the
are	his	have	of	a
that	be	with	was	this
it	from	I	you	for

Dr. Fry's Instant Words Bingo
Card A-21

SET **A**

Instant Words 1–25

have	was	with	be	is
his	for	this	and	you
at	from	it	in	are
the	I	he	as	to
they	on	a	that	of

a	that	on	have	they
with	is	was	of	be
for	you	and	his	this
it	in	the	are	to
he	from	at	as	I

to	he	and	is	they
as	I	you	be	on
at	from	for	with	that
a	was	it	this	in
the	are	his	of	have

28

he	was	on	for	you
they	with	as	I	to
and	have	from	at	are
be	in	that	his	is
this	a	of	the	it

Dr. Fry's Instant Words Bingo
Card A-25

SET **A**
Instant Words 1–25

with	for	from	at	as
to	he	and	is	they
that	on	be	you	I
have	of	his	in	this
it	was	a	the	are

Set B: Instant Words 26–50

or	but	we	there	she
one	not	when	use	do
had	what	your	an ✓	how
by	all	can ✓	each	their
words	were	said	which	if

Directions

1. Duplicate one Bingo card for each student. Each student needs a different Bingo card, but all Bingo cards must be from the same set.

2. Call out the words in the word list above in any order—first to last, then at another time last to first, etc.

3. As you call each word, use it in a sentence or phrase, then repeat the word.

4. Ask the students to mark an **X** on top of each word that is called.

5. Allow sufficient time for the students to search for the word on their Bingo cards before saying the next word.

6. Remember to omit two words if you are using the game for diagnosis. (See Round 2: Diagnostic Bingo on page 3.) As the students learn the words, the rate of calling out the words can be increased.

When you are teaching beginning readers, you can write the word on the board or hold up a flash card containing the word so the students can make a visual match. The same Instant Words are available on flash cards from Teacher Created Materials or at educational school supply stores, or you can make your own flash cards. After students become more familiar with the Instant Words, you can just call out the words (without writing on the board or using flash cards).

Do not proceed to the next set until most of the students have learned the majority of the words. Generally speaking, Set C and Set D are too advanced for kindergarten. However, all sets are suitable for first grade, second grade, and remedial or ELL students.

Save the student cards for individualized instruction, a record of progress, and take-home evidence of learning.

or	one	had	by	words
but	not	what	were	all
we	when	your	can	said
there	use	an	each	which
she	do	how	their	if

or	but	we	there	she
one	not	when	use	do
had	what	an	your	how
by	were	can	their	each
words	all	said	if	which

had	what	your	an	how
by	were	can	each	their
words	all	said	which	if
or	but	we	there	she
one	not	when	use	do

words	all	said	which	if
or	but	we	there	she
one	not	when	use	do
had	what	your	an	how
by	were	can	each	their

Dr. Fry's Instant Words Bingo

Card B-5

SET **B**

Instant Words 26–50

which	each	how	do	she
if	their	your	use	there
said	can	an	when	we
all	were	what	not	but
words	or	by	had	one

Dr. Fry's Instant Words Bingo

Card B-6

SET **B**

Instant Words 26–50

if	how	she	each	an
there	can	when	were	what
but	by	one	or	had
words	not	all	we	your
which	do	their	said	use

she	there	we	but	or
do	use	when	not	one
how	an	what	had	your
their	each	can	were	by
if	which	said	all	words

how	each	said	which	their
if	do	an	can	all
words	were	your	use	she
there	when	what	by	had
not	we	but	one	or

Dr. Fry's Instant Words Bingo

SET **B**

Instant Words 26–50

words	all	by	said	were
had	one	what	can	which
if	each	an	when	or
but	their	she	do	there
we	use	how	your	not

their	if	do	how	she
which	each	an	use	there
said	can	your	when	we
all	were	what	not	but
words	by	had	one	or

when	we	said	your	can
not	but	all	were	what
one	or	words	by	had
use	there	which	each	an
do	she	if	their	how

Dr. Fry's Instant Words Bingo

Card B-12

there	she	we	but	one
had	not	when	use	do
by	what	an	your	how
or	were	can	their	each
all	words	which	if	said

use	there	which	each	an
their	do	she	if	how
your	can	when	said	we
what	not	were	but	all
had	by	one	words	or

Dr. Fry's Instant Words Bingo

Card B-14

SET **B**

Instant Words 26–50

do	use	she	if	there
when	not	we	which	their
how	each	said	but	one
or	all	can	an	your
were	words	by	what	had

Dr. Fry's Instant Words Bingo

Card B-15

SET **B**

Instant Words 26–50

an	can	when	we	said
were	what	not	but	all
each	do	she	how	which
or	one	words	by	had
your	use	there	their	if

Dr. Fry's Instant Words Bingo

Card B-16

how	do	she	there	we
but	one	had	by	or
words	all	said	if	which
each	their	your	use	when
not	what	were	can	an

but	not	what	were	all
said	we	when	can	an
their	if	your	there	use
do	she	how	each	which
had	by	words	one	or

Dr. Fry's Instant Words Bingo

Card B-18

SET **B**

Instant Words 26–50

your	what	had	how	an
use	do	not	one	when
we	but	or	she	there
which	if	words	all	said
were	can	each	their	by

if	said	words	all	which
can	each	their	by	were
your	an	how	what	had
use	when	do	one	not
there	she	or	but	we

Dr. Fry's Instant Words Bingo

Card B-20

SET **B**

Instant Words 26–50

but	all	were	what	not
can	when	we	said	your
use	there	which	an	each
if	she	do	how	their
or	words	one	had	by

said	can	your	an	each
which	how	their	if	all
were	what	words	by	had
she	do	use	there	when
we	but	not	or	one

Dr. Fry's Instant Words Bingo

Card B-22

SET **B**

Instant Words 26–50

do	not	one	when	use
but	or	there	she	we
if	which	said	all	words
their	each	were	can	by
what	your	how	an	had

there	do	she	we	use
how	words	or	all	said
were	by	had	what	can
if	which	their	an	not
one	but	when	your	each

can	an	said	when	we
if	their	your	use	there
she	do	how	each	which
but	not	what	were	all
words	by	had	one	or

Dr. Fry's Instant Words Bingo

Card B-25

SET **B**

Instant Words 26–50

or	there	she	we	but
can	an	said	when	use
your	their	if	do	what
each	which	all	one	had
words	by	not	how	were

Set C: Instant Words 51–75

will	many	some	him	two
up	then	her	into	more
other	them	would	time	write
about	these	make	has	go
out	so	like	look	see

Directions

1. Duplicate one Bingo card for each student. Each student needs a different Bingo card, but all Bingo cards must be from the same set.

2. Call out the words in the word list above in any order—first to last, then at another time last to first, etc.

3. As you call each word, use it in a sentence or phrase, then repeat the word.

4. Ask the students to mark an **X** on top of each word that is called.

5. Allow sufficient time for the students to search for the word on their Bingo cards before saying the next word.

6. Remember to omit two words if you are using the game for diagnosis. (See Round 2: Diagnostic Bingo on page 3.) As the students learn the words, the rate of calling out the words can be increased.

When you are teaching beginning readers, you can write the word on the board or hold up a flash card containing the word so the students can make a visual match. The same Instant Words are available on flash cards from Teacher Created Materials or at educational school supply stores, or you can make your own flash cards. After students become more familiar with the Instant Words, you can just call out the words (without writing on the board or using flash cards).

Do not proceed to the next set until most of the students have learned the majority of the words. Generally speaking, Set C and Set D are too advanced for kindergarten. However, all sets are suitable for first grade, second grade, and remedial or ELL students.

Save the student cards for individualized instruction, a record of progress, and take-home evidence of learning.

will	up	other	about	out
many	then	them	these	so
some	her	would	make	like
him	into	time	has	look
two	more	write	go	see

out	so	like	look	see
more	into	her	then	up
other	them	would	time	write
will	many	some	him	two
about	these	make	has	go

Dr. Fry's Instant Words Bingo

Card C-3

SET **C**

Instant Words 51–75

about	these	make	has	go
out	so	like	look	see
write	time	would	them	other
more	into	her	then	up
will	many	some	two	him

60

© Teacher Created Materials, Inc.

up	then	her	into	more
will	two	many	some	him
time	would	them	other	write
about	go	has	make	these
see	out	so	like	look

Dr. Fry's Instant Words Bingo

Card C-5

has	go	make	these	about
out	so	like	look	see
more	her	into	then	up
many	will	him	some	two
other	them	would	time	write

see	go	write	more	two
look	has	time	into	him
like	make	would	some	her
so	these	them	then	many
out	about	up	will	other

see	write	two	has	into
like	make	her	these	then
out	other	will	up	about
many	them	so	some	would
him	time	look	more	go

up	will	about	other	many
out	them	then	so	these
her	some	would	make	him
like	time	into	look	has
two	more	see	go	write

so	these	them	then	many
out	about	other	up	will
see	go	write	more	two
some	her	would	make	like
him	into	time	has	look

into	see	time	go	write
more	two	look	has	him
like	would	make	her	some
so	these	then	them	many
about	out	other	up	will

about	other	up	will	out
then	many	them	so	these
some	would	her	like	make
time	into	him	has	look
write	go	see	two	more

Dr. Fry's Instant Words Bingo
SET C
Card C-12

Instant Words 51–75

will	see	up	go	other
write	more	about	out	two
look	many	then	has	time
them	these	into	him	so
some	her	would	make	like

so	like	time	two	make
other	go	out	has	him
some	would	them	look	write
will	see	more	many	these
her	up	about	then	into

Dr. Fry's Instant Words Bingo

Card C-14

see	more	many	these	her
will	write	look	them	some
other	two	time	so	like
go	out	has	him	make
up	about	then	into	would

Dr. Fry's Instant Words Bingo

SET **C**

Instant Words 51–75

then	many	look	has	two
into	these	write	him	make
time	about	more	them	out
up	see	will	go	like
her	would	some	so	other

72

Dr. Fry's Instant Words Bingo

Card C-16

SET **C**

Instant Words 51–75

like	so	them	some	these
her	would	make	him	into
up	go	out	has	about
then	time	other	two	will
write	look	see	many	more

Dr. Fry's Instant Words Bingo
Card C-17

SET C
Instant Words 51–75

make	like	him	into	time
has	look	two	more	write
go	see	would	her	some
these	so	then	many	them
will	out	about	other	up

74

© Teacher Created Materials, Inc.

Dr. Fry's Instant Words Bingo
Card C-18

SET **C**

Instant Words 51–75

these	some	so	would	her
make	him	like	into	time
look	has	two	write	more
go	see	will	up	other
about	out	many	then	them

Dr. Fry's Instant Words Bingo
Card C-19

will	these	go	has	make
out	so	see	look	like
him	two	then	would	about
other	many	more	into	her
time	write	some	them	up

them	up	some	write	time
into	more	other	many	her
then	would	about	two	him
like	out	see	look	so
go	has	make	will	these

other	up	about	will	out
them	these	then	so	some
would	her	make	him	like
into	has	time	look	two
more	write	go	see	many

Dr. Fry's Instant Words Bingo

Card C-22

him	her	time	write	some
up	them	into	more	other
many	two	would	about	then
so	go	has	out	see
look	these	make	will	like

would	about	then	him	two
her	many	more	into	other
them	some	up	time	write
out	see	like	so	look
has	go	these	make	will

Dr. Fry's Instant Words Bingo

Card C-24

SET **C**

Instant Words 51–75

about	many	some	see	go
will	look	write	other	two
make	so	time	into	him
these	like	more	up	then
has	out	would	them	her

him	into	time	has	look
two	more	write	go	see
will	up	other	about	many
out	then	these	them	some
so	her	would	make	like

Set D: Instant Words 76–100

number	my	call	find	get
no	than	who	long	come
way	first	am	down	made
could	water	its	day	may
people	been	now	did	part

Directions

1. Duplicate one Bingo card for each student. Each student needs a different Bingo card, but all Bingo cards must be from the same set.

2. Call out the words in the word list above in any order—first to last, then at another time last to first, etc.

3. As you call each word, use it in a sentence or phrase, then repeat the word.

4. Ask the students to mark an **X** on top of each word that is called.

5. Allow sufficient time for the students to search for the word on their Bingo cards before saying the next word.

6. Remember to omit two words if you are using the game for diagnosis. (See Round 2: Diagnostic Bingo on page 3.) As the students learn the words, the rate of calling out the words can be increased.

   When you are teaching beginning readers, you can write the word on the board or hold up a flash card containing the word so the students can make a visual match. The same Instant Words are available on flash cards from Teacher Created Materials or at educational school supply stores, or you can make your own flash cards. After students become more familiar with the Instant Words, you should just call out the words (without writing on the board or using flash cards).

Do not proceed to the next set until most of the students have learned a majority of the words. Generally speaking, Set C and Set D are too advanced for kindergarten. However, all sets are suitable for first grade, second grade, and remedial or ELL students.

Save the student cards for individualized instruction, a record of progress, and take-home evidence of learning.

Dr. Fry's Instant Words Bingo

number	no	way	could	people
my	than	first	water	been
call	who	am	its	now
find	long	down	day	did
get	come	made	may	part

Dr. Fry's Instant Words Bingo

SET **D**

Instant Words 76–100

my	number	call	find	get
no	who	than	long	come
way	first	down	am	made
could	water	its	day	may
been	people	now	part	did

#3523 Instant Words Bingo

may	day	its	water	could
part	did	now	been	people
get	find	call	my	number
come	long	who	than	no
made	way	first	am	down

did	may	made	come	part
get	day	am	find	long
now	its	than	down	call
number	people	water	first	who
could	been	way	my	no

part	may	made	come	get
did	day	down	long	find
its	been	who	am	call
water	first	than	people	my
way	now	could	number	no

Dr. Fry's Instant Words Bingo

SET **D**

Instant Words 76–100

no	could	people	than	water
call	am	now	long	day
get	made	part	may	come
did	down	find	its	who
been	first	my	way	number

Dr. Fry's Instant Words Bingo
Card D-7

Instant Words 76–100

come	day	water	number	who
been	did	get	call	no
could	made	am	down	first
my	find	now	part	people
way	its	may	long	than

Dr. Fry's Instant Words Bingo

Card D-8

SET **D**

Instant Words 76–100

who	number	come	day	than
water	people	way	no	call
get	did	been	first	my
could	find	its	may	long
now	am	made	part	down

Dr. Fry's Instant Words Bingo

Card D-9

SET **D**

Instant Words 76–100

its	now	find	long	down
day	did	get	come	made
may	part	number	no	way
could	people	my	than	first
water	been	call	who	am

may	part	made	come	did
get	down	day	long	find
its	now	who	am	call
been	first	water	than	my
could	people	no	way	number

down	part	am	made	long
now	may	its	find	way
than	day	come	number	who
people	water	no	could	call
did	get	first	my	been

Dr. Fry's Instant Words Bingo

Card D-12

SET **D**

Instant Words 76–100

my	than	been	water	first
who	call	its	am	now
long	find	down	did	day
get	come	may	made	part
people	could	way	number	no

may	no	number	part	way
made	come	could	people	get
did	my	than	day	down
first	water	long	find	been
who	call	am	its	now

its	now	call	am	who
number	part	way	may	no
could	people	get	come	made
than	my	did	down	day
water	first	been	long	find

Dr. Fry's Instant Words Bingo

SET **D**

Card D-15

Instant Words 76–100

day	find	made	who	no
am	may	come	down	long
call	way	get	did	been
first	part	my	people	now
than	water	could	its	number

Dr. Fry's Instant Words Bingo

Card D-16

SET D

Instant Words 76–100

first	been	long	find	day
made	no	who	am	call
now	its	number	could	than
water	part	way	may	come
down	did	get	people	my

way	get	number	who	long
people	may	could	am	find
day	call	than	come	my
did	part	its	no	been
water	down	first	now	made

Dr. Fry's Instant Words Bingo

Card D-18

SET **D**

Instant Words 76–100

people	my	could	way	no
number	water	first	than	been
its	am	call	who	now
down	long	find	day	did
part	made	come	get	may

Dr. Fry's Instant Words Bingo
Card D-19

SET **D**

Instant Words 76–100

been	no	made	did	now
get	day	who	way	than
come	find	first	call	could
may	my	water	am	long
down	part	people	number	its